101 Ways to Love Your Husband

*Practical Ways to Love
and Encourage Your Husband*

Introduction

I've noticed something about this species we call "men." We might look tough, act tough, want to be tough, etc. . . . But deep down we're softies who want our wives to baby and pamper us with kindness and love!

Ladies, please let these practical ideas come to life in your relationship with your husband. You will have fun together and experience the oneness that Christ desires for your marriage.

Respect Him

You say, "I can't because he . . ." Stop the critical thinking. Focus on one area where you respect him and begin to encourage him in this area. Your positive comments will generate more positive thoughts, and hopefully, the cycle will continue.

Keep
the Car Clean

For some wives, the house is their castle and the car is their pig sty. For husbands it is generally the opposite. Just as you expect him to help you keep the house clean, so you should also help him keep the car clean.

Comb His Hair

S ome evening ask him to lay his head in your lap and, as you watch a TV show or read a book, gently brush through his hair to relax him. God has blessed you with love for each other. It is a divine gift from Him. You are the only lady who can — and should — share this beautiful moment with your husband.

Pray For Him

S ure, it's been said thousands of times, but you need to be reminded to pray for him. Do it when he's down and when he's up. He needs your prayers every day. You are a great source of strength to him through Christ.

Practice
Ephesians 5:22-23

"Wives, submit to your husbands as to the Lord. For the husband is the head of the wife as Christ is the head of the church, his body, of which he is the Savior." Submission is not a popular word in our society, but a truly biblical submission is critical to the task of building a loving relationship.

Challenge His Physical Condition

One of the best ways to love your hubby is to make sure he takes care of himself. If you see him abusing his body by overworking, overeating, lack of exercise, etc., seek to lovingly encourage him to care for his body. Don't nag . . . just encourage.

Sing

That's right. Around the home . . . just sing. Let your life be a melodious song echoing through the house. By creating a mood of joy you will potentially disarm his tensions. Who knows? He may join you for a duet.

Remember Proverbs 27:15

"Aquarrelsome wife is like a constant dripping on a rainy day; restraining her is like restraining the wind or grasping oil with the hand." Have you ever tried to hold a cup of cooking oil in your bare hand. Impossible. Try it! If you're a quarrelsome wife, that's what it's like for your husband to try to hold you — so change!

Time Away

E very couple needs time away with each other. Remind your husband of the joy you have when you have that private, focused time. Make sure plans are made for an upcoming experience together. It is especially difficult to plan these times when the children are young, but it is also critical that you take time now to build your relationship and keep it top priority.

Be Forgiving

Colossians 3:12-13 encourages us to forgive others just as we desire to be forgiven. If you are holding something against your husband or keeping score in some area, forgive that right now. Let the score be zero to zero and keep it there. Your marriage is not a competition — it's a relationship.

Surprise Him
at Work

S how up at his workplace with a bouquet of flowers or balloons. That's right, husbands like surprises, too. It's the 90s! Get with it . . . bring us flowers!!!

Hide Chocolate

P ut chocolate candy under his pillow and when you're both in bed say, "Honey, would you like a BIG surprise tonight?" When he leans over, anticipating what's to come, tell him to reach under his pillow. You'll both laugh, then hopefully do some other stuff!?!?!?!?!

Love What He Loves

Know the things that are important to him, the things that get his attention and in which he places value. Join him in that placement of value. It is pleasing to the Lord, and you will become more unified in your relationship.

Is He Lonely?

I f your husband is lonely, seek to bring couples and friends into your life that will help him develop relationships with other men. Pray for the Lord to send someone into his life to be an accountability partner and encourager.

Be a Titus Woman

Titus 2:4-5 encourages women to love their husbands and children, to be self-controlled and pure, to be busy at home, to be kind, and to be subject to their husbands. Look at the reason they are to do this: "So that no one will malign the word of God." Your love for your husband is designed to be an outreach of Scripture.

Allow Openness and Honesty

Most men have some secrets they are afraid to share with their wives. They are afraid that if they open up, they will look foolish or be misunderstood. If your husband ventures to share something very personal, seek to be understanding and not judgmental. If your girlfriend called to reveal the same thing, how would you respond to her? Probably with care and understanding. How much more, then, does your husband deserve that love?

Let It Go!

You know — that one little thing you do that drives him nuts. The one that's caused countless arguments. Let it GO! Stop doing it! If you don't, it's only going to cause more frustration and grief.

Back to the Basics

Why did you fall in love with your husband? Take time to recall your first few dates together. Are those same flames still burning? If so, be thankful and continue to burn together. If not, please go back and practice something you did in the beginning. Go out on a date just like in ol' times. Go parking! Do something dramatic!

Just a Big Kid

B asically, men are just big children. They need the same things children need: love, encouragement, someone to moan to when they're sick. Don't tell him you're doing it, but love him like a kid. . . .

Benefit
Of the Doubt

Instead of assuming where your husband is headed in a conversation or assuming why he took a certain action, let him have the opportunity to explain his reasons for his behavior. Then seek to understand it from his perspective. Work at being an attentive listener!

A to Z

Give your husband a list of qualities you see in his life that are beautiful to you. Starting with A and going to Z, give him 26 compliments.

Never Use Always

I n those silly little arguments with your husband that are always bigger than they ought to be, make sure you don't say things like: "You *always* do this or you *always* do that." If your husband is sincerely seeking to change, an "always" remark will only discourage him, possibly causing him to give up.

Kisses Along the Way, Will Really Make His Day

Greet him with a kiss. Say goodbye with a kiss. Go to bed with a kiss. Say thanks with a kiss. Just kiss! Become a kissaholic.

Look Your Best

The special times you share together are the most important times to look your very best. When you date or attend an engagement together, look your sharpest. If you have a job outside the home, you leave for work each day looking neatly dressed and attractive. Give that same effort (and beyond) for the special times you share with your husband. Make a statement of love to your husband by your personal appearance.

Clown Around

H ave fun together. Sometimes just be silly and roll on the floor or play along with his silly games. Laugh. Touch. Smile. Tickle.

Let Love Win

Determine in your heart that you will always love your husband. Your marriage commitment was "for better, for worse, till death do us part." When it's better, let love win. When it's worse . . . let love win!!

Buy Something Skimpy!

Yea, just for fun! Buy the thing you least like — and he'll probably love it. Model it for him. It's okay . . . you're married. You're the only one who can share this with him. (Don't let him see this book first; he'll probably suggest you start with this one.)

Practice Your Preaching

Make sure you do the things you ask your husband to do. In other words, if you ask him to be patient, practice patience with him. If you ask him to trust, be trusting. If you ask him to forgive, be forgiving. If you ask . . .

Dinner Delight

One day, for no particular reason other than love, prepare his favorite meal, dessert and all. To make it even more special, call him thirty minutes before he is to arrive and let him know you can't wait until he gets home because you've got a surprise for him. If you can't prepare the meal at home, take him to his favorite restaurant and enjoy dinner together. Use this special time to say loving things to each other.

Massage Therapy

G ive him a full body or neck massage. Go all out. Your caring, loving touch will create harmony. Your efforts to relax him and relieve stress will hopefully make him more responsive to your needs.

Help Him
With a Project

Find out what project he's working on at the office or at home and offer a helping hand. Be a partner in life's experiences.

Love Notes

Get into the habit of writing one a week. Leave it in his planner or lunch box. If he goes on a trip, put little sticky notes throughout his clothes. Notes are special because they reflect effort and time given to him.

Hobby Heaven

Here's a great idea. You know his hobby, right? Do it with him — even suggest it when he's not expecting it. Go have fun together. It's possible you might begin enjoying the same hobby.

Leave and Cleave

If you have a tendency to rely on your mom or dad when you should rely on the willing strength of your husband — change! Relying on parents can seriously harm both parties. The Bible specifically teaches parental separation because it's the way to carry on the work of the Lord from generation to generation. Without doubt parents are a blessing from the Lord, but they are not *one* with you. That identity belongs to your husband. Obey Scripture.

Free Him Up

If your husband has a very busy work schedule and diligently seeks to give time to you and the family, seek to free his schedule for some fun, relaxing times. He will greatly appreciate your sensitivity to his work and responsibility load, and the rest he receives will renew his strength.

Insist on Dates

Make sure you consistently plan dates together. Every couple needs to be alone, enjoying times together untouched by elements that put demands on their schedules. Ask him to date you. Set aside cash to help finance these times. Look for ways to spend more time together.

Build Hedges

Be careful in your relationships with other men and women. Do not let others break into your relationship with your husband. If you sense your desires are building toward a third party, RUN! Keep up strong defenses against these outside forces. Pray that the Lord will help you recognize them as they come against you.

Tear Down Walls

If there is a wall between you and your husband, do your part to knock away some bricks. Don't wait for him to start — go first! No doubt several bricks have been placed there from your side anyway. Walls become rooms, rooms become buildings, buildings become towers, towers become cities . . . GOD HELP US AS COUPLES!

Soak It Up

Some men seldom pay compliments to their wives. If you live with this kind of man, when he *does* say something nice, soak it up. Tell him how much the compliment means to you. Then, don't place unrealistic expectations on him. Let him continue to grow and develop in this area.

Rise Above It All

Never let Satan discourage you to the point of giving up. Maybe you want more from your husband. Maybe you've asked for more from your husband. Let your hope and joy be in Christ. As Habakkuk 3:18 says, "I will rejoice in the Lord, I will be joyful in God my Savior." You have a greater hope — rise to it today.

Watch for Signs

Don't be naive. If your husband is unusually quiet, ask questions. If he shows a decreased desire to be around you, ask why. If his mood toward you is different, speak to him about it. Don't wait until it's too late. Talk with him about his thoughts and feelings NOW. Your relationship's survival depends on it.

Practice
Proverbs 31:12

This passage says that a wife of noble character brings her husband "good, not harm, all the days of her life." Think of your actions this week. Have they brought good to your husband and your family? What a challenge!

Know His Needs and Meet Them

Take time to share with your husband that you desire to meet his needs. Then ask how you can fulfill what he perceives as his top three needs. Don't look surprised or react negatively to his suggestions. As you can, seek to meet those needs . . . hopefully he will ask for yours as well. (If he doesn't, leave him a little note listing them anyway.)

Initiate It

Okay, we all know one of his top three needs will be something in the physical area! That's not only normal, it's true according to all surveys. So . . . initiate some physical encounters. When he arrives home from work, tell him you can't wait to be with him later on in the evening. Build up his ego a bit . . . it's okay.

List His Top Ten!

Make a list of the top ten qualities you love about your husband. Post them in a prominent place in your home. Point to them and have fun with him. He will love it!!

Since You Know His Weakness

B e sure to encourage and support him in prayer in this critical area. So many times we focus on the weakness and only make the problem worse. According to Scripture, you are one flesh, so accept the problem as your own and treat it with love and care.

Compliment Him in Public

When the opportunities arise, share complimentary statements about your husband when you're out with family and friends. Talk openly about your love and admiration for him. Find the good and celebrate it. Doing this builds your relationship and gives good role modeling to others.

Become More Knowledgeable

There is probably some sport or hobby your husband enjoys that you're "clueless" about (i.e., golf, football, card collecting, airplanes, etc.). Read up on it. Surprise him by asking questions that make sense! Show interest in his world.

Die to Self

The very opposite of God is "the self." Satan would love to get you focused on your own agenda and your own desires, leaving God and your husband "out in the cold." Pray for wisdom from God to recognize selfishness and obediently seek to cleanse it from your life. Think of one area today that needs cleaning . . . act on it.

Moving?

I s your family preparing to move? So much anxiety and change are involved in such an experience. Try to keep the stress level low through the move by relying on the Lord for strength. Seek to be a helpful partner and not a complainer as you go through the process.

Act On What You Know

B efore you ever read one idea in this little book, you knew a way you could love your husband. Do that . . . start with what you already know. If you never act, things never change.

Remember . . .

The more consistent you are in your devotions and prayer, the more you normally think on godly things. The deeper you grow in Christ, the more joyful your life will be. The more joyful your life is, the more of a delight you will be to your husband.

Job Change?

Is your husband facing a job change or a possible termination? This is a devastating experience for most men. He will probably be more edgy and short with you and other family members as he goes through this tough transition. Seek to understand the stress and challenge he is facing.

Special Treats

This idea is such a delight for a man. Sometime, when he's just talking about something he would like to eat, surprise him by going and making it for him right then. It's best if he doesn't know about it at all and walks in on you just completing the project. If you have kids, let them be in on the surprise and help you stall him in other areas of the home. When he gets to the kitchen — surprise! — what he's wanted is right there! WOW!

Listen . . .

Normally, women are better listeners than men. Sometimes men attempt to communicate deeper issues, but don't know how. Listen for these "deeper" issues. Try to help your husband communicate. Ask questions, then give him freedom to respond honestly and openly.

Kiss Him
Like Crazy

Just go wild sometimes. Kiss his head, kiss his cheek, kiss his lips, kiss his hands . . . kiss him all over . . . be silly, have fun . . . life goes by quickly.

On Long Trips

The next time you go on a trip, buy some of his favorite treats and put them in the glove compartment or another concealed place in the car. After a while, reach in and pull out a surprise to keep him awake and focused. He'll love this little touch of love you add to the journey.

Believe in Yourself

You are a gift from God to your husband. If you tend to think negatively about yourself and your gifts — stop. God has put you into a relationship with another one of His children. You have much to offer and He will cause your strengths to blossom as you joyfully believe in what He already has given you.

Clothe Yourself
with Proverbs 31:25

"She is clothed with strength and dignity." Two powerful items. [Strength — that only comes from Christ. And dignity, which is godly professionalism.] Let these two ingredients be part of the mixture that blends to make you beautiful.

Sit on His Lap

When you have the opportunity, sit gently in his lap — not a "plop, plop" kind of sit, but a tender, caring, loving-arms-around-his-neck sit. It's a great way to communicate your love for each other and reflect the unity you have in your spirits.

Shower with Him

When you hear him in the shower, quietly enter the bathroom, disrobe and join him in the shower for a great time of relaxing and being together. Enjoy these pleasurable moments together. (LOCK THE DOOR!)

Don't Panic

If you have the tendency to panic when unexpected news comes your way, work on changing. Your husband may fear telling you certain things because of your reactions. Your panic could be harming communication.

At-Home Cooking

If you typically take care of the cooking, invite your husband to help you prepare the evening meals. It's a great occasion to share conversation and be teammates. Also, most husbands love those "at-home" meals and this will help him understand what it takes to put it all together.

Don't Call Him "Babysitter"

If you have young children and plan on going out for the evening — leaving your husband with the kids — don't call him a "babysitter." He's DAD! These are his children too. You are not a babysitter and he is not a babysitter — you are parents!!

Weave

We are taught in Ecclesiastes 4:9-12 the value of intricately weaving our lives together. Can you think of a cord in your own life today that needs to be bound to your husband? If so, weave today and share your intentions with him.

Cleave

Don't run to mommy every time you disagree with your husband. You're an adult. Cleave to your spouse and make decisions together. If your husband isn't making godly decisions and will not let you be a part of the process, seek some type of counseling. Few parents have the ability to give their grown children unbiased guidance — and that is what you need.

Play Games

C hallenge him to a game of one-on-one or a fun board game. Have a reward planned for the winner. Create friendly, healthy competition.

No Mind Games

The only game you shouldn't play with your husband is "the mind game." Be careful not to let your experience in controlling situations and use of body language selfishly manipulate your husband's decisions. Some women have "the gift" in this area and aren't afraid to use it. It will not benefit your marriage.

Go to Bed Early

Ask your husband to join you for an early evening retirement. Pour a glass of his favorite drink and enjoy relaxing and talking in bed. If you'd like, let it lead to other stuff. . . .

Accept Him

Romans 15:7 states, "Accept one another, then, just as Christ accepted you, in order to bring praise to God." It's obvious we're all different. Sometimes it seems the person we married is totally opposite to us — more than anyone else in the world. Scripture doesn't cut us any slack; we are to seek to accept those differences and use them to help us mature in our walk with each other and with Christ. Don't relax your standards in biblical truths, but accept each other in non-eternal differences.

Read to Him

A sk him to choose a favorite book and invite him to lie on the couch with his head in your lap as you read it to him. This definitely requires servanthood, but it will be a wonderful experience in unifying you.

Write a Poem

Create some heartfelt, beautiful phrases about your husband and put them on paper. Write them out or print them and frame the result. Give this personally enhanced gift to your husband as a special addition to his office or workroom.

On His Birthday

Do lots of special things. Let surprises come at him from all directions. Keep one final surprise for bedtime or possibly give it to him the next morning. Tell him every day should be a special day for him. Build him up.

Buy His Favorite Magazine

O rder a magazine he enjoys that you don't currently receive. Obviously only do this if you're in good financial condition.

Be Real

Don't "fake" your love. Let him know your inner thoughts and seek to help him understand you and your methods of communication. He may desire to have you communicate your love in other ways. Discover those ways and enhance your own communication skills.

Keep a Balance

B͟e a well-balanced individual by maintaining growth and symmetry in emotional, physical, spiritual and mental disciplines. Let him suggest areas in which he feels you need to grow and if there is truth in his statements, be open to the Holy Spirit.

Watch Out for Materialism

It's easy to compare what you have with the neighbors. It's easy to want what they have. It's even easy to wish your husband made as much as they do . . . STOP! WAIT A MINUTE! What are we after? If you have love, you have much more than most in our world have. Celebrate what you have.

He Is Priority

Many wives view their children as more important than their husbands. It may be that they are more dependent on you than your husband, but they are not more important. The Bible teaches the importance of excellent parenting, but it never places the children at a higher priority level than the spouse. In fact, because you are "one flesh," it is literally impossible to be more intimate with your children than you are with your marriage partner. "Train up a child in the way he should go," we are told (Prov. 22:6 NASB). And they *will* eventually go. You, however, will stay. And so will he. The relationship between you and him takes first priority.

Kill the "Zingers"

One negative comment to your husband will offset twenty-five wonderful statements you have already made. Work at speaking "kind" to your mate. See how long you can go without saying anything that will harm him.

Write a Memory

O n this page . . . write down a wonderful memory you've
shared with your mate. Enjoy thinking about it.

Apologize

If you're wrong, say it. Stubbornness is simply selfishness. Selfishness is a marriage destroyer. Apologize . . . NOW!

Walk It Off

If you're frustrated with something that has happened in the home, go for a walk or find another way to release the tension from your body. Exercise always helps!

Be "Home" for Him

Without you, your house is nothing more than wood, nails and man-made materials. You are what makes home "home." You are a treasure. You are the element that turns that wooden structure into a place of love. Consider yourself his "home."

Put Your Face in a Place

Take a picture of yourself and put it in a place where he looks every day. Let him see you smiling back at him. Keep "you" in front of him. Make sure you pick out one that is uniquely you. . . .

Shine Like a Star

Philippians 2:14-15 encourages us to do everything without complaining or arguing so we can "shine like stars" and claim that our life was not a labor in vain. Keep the big picture in mind. We are to do everything to honor God. Let your marriage shine!

Banner of Love

Make a banner to hang across a room in the house or even on the outside of the house. On it, write a slogan for your husband. (Example: I LOVE YOU _____, WORLD'S BEST HUBBY!) Have fun watching his face when he arrives home. If you have children, let them help make the banner.

Take a Picture

Without him knowing, plan to have a professional picture taken of you or, if it applies, the children. Again, you're showing him you think of him and also his mind will think of you every time he sees it.

Serve

Think of a lady in your life who has been a godly example of servanthood. Think of the respect and admiration you have for her. When she is gone, what will people say about her? Hopefully, you also want that testimony to be said about you. Live now to earn the respect and love of those around you and be a model of servanthood.

Practice Proverbs 31:20

I t states, "She opens her arms to the poor and extends her hands to the needy." Portraying this scriptural challenge will be an example to your husband and will challenge him to live the same type of lifestyle.

Attitude Check

Are you always ready to "offer a word of praise"? Sometimes when you find yourself with a grumpy spirit, stop and give yourself an attitude check. Decide to be positive — and just do it!

Unique Cookies

Bake some cookies and write little love phrases on each one. Make hearts with your names on them. Attempt to decorate one by drawing a picture of yourself on it.

Rent a Movie

Go together and pick out a romantic movie to share in the comfort of your own home. Make popcorn and chill some sparkling grape juice. Cuddle. Bring pillows and blankets to the couch. Fall asleep after the movie in the warmth of each other's arms.

Wear His Shirts

Many husbands love for their wives to wear their shirts to sleep in, relax around the house in, etc. I believe this gives an intimate sense of closeness which only a husband and wife should and can share. Ask your husband if he would like this, then try it!

Cut the Grass

Do this or some other "around the house" chore that you don't normally do. Surprise him by having it done and encourage him to spend that extra time doing something fun with you. Make some suggestions or ask for his ideas.

Remember
Psalm 139:17-18

"How precious to me are your thoughts, O God! How vast is the sum of them! Were I to count them, they would outnumber the grains of sand. When I awake, I am still with you." God is watching over you and thinking of you constantly. He is there to bring you strength and comfort, and today He wants to bless your life with His goodness.

101 Ways to Love Your Wife

Get him the counterpart to this little book. It's just for husbands and it will give him great ideas and challenges.

Living Bible

B e a constant example of Scripture. Let your husband's favorite version of Scripture be your life because of your consistent, faithful walk and talk.

Iron His Shirts

When he's going to a function that requires sharp dressing, help him look his best by getting the wrinkles out of his clothes. The better he looks, the better you look.

In the Word

Of all the things you will ever do, there's no doubt that the most important is to be a woman who reads and applies the Bible to your everyday life. It will at times be exciting. Other times it may be incredibly boring and mundane. The issue is not excitement or boredom — it's consistency. You must read the Bible to increase in knowledge and understanding. Be accountable and faithful in this most important area.

Spend
100 Seconds

Holding his face between your hands, looking into his eyes, telling him you love him. Stare into his eyes. Look deeply. One hundred seconds will feel like a long time, even uncomfortable. But how often do we stop to simply let our focus be on each other? Do it for 100 seconds.

Never Stop

L ove always perseveres. After giving, serving, loving, caring . . . turn right around and start doing it again. Love is more than a feeling — it is a process. Please, with the help of Christ, enjoy and continue the process.